THE SPIRIT OF GIVING

Fidelis Osamusali

Copyright © 2010 by Fidelis Osamusali

The Spirit of Giving
by Fidelis Osamusali

Printed in the United States of America

ISBN 9781609579210

All rights reserved solely by the author. The author guarantees all contents are original and do not infringe upon the legal rights of any other person or work. No part of this book may be reproduced in any form without the permission of the author. The views expressed in this book are not necessarily those of the publisher.

Unless otherwise indicated, Bible quotations are taken from The Holy Bible, New King James Version. Copyright © 1982 by Thomas Nelson, Inc.

www.xulonpress.com

PREFACE

The Lord gave me this prophetic word "The curse is broken, the Blessing is released, and the name of the Lord is glorified" a few years ago, as He birth in me this revelation of the Spirit of Giving.

The Word says that The Blessing of the Lord makes rich; it adds no sorrow to it. It is my true belief and conviction that as you read and take in the contents of this book "The Spirit of Giving" there would literally come upon you a new understanding, which would release a great manifestation of The Blessing of the Lord in your life, going forward.

It is my prayer that this book would enlighten you, firm you up, establish you and develop a strong vision of the word and anointing of the spirit of giving in your life, to new levels and to new heights in Jesus name. Amen.

Table of Contents

Introduction ix
In times like these 13
The Spirit of Giving 20
The Blessing of the Lord..36
The Spirit of Liberality 42
Giving Produces Results..52
Hearing and Obeying His Voice..............................64
Receiving by Grace..72
Conclusion 83
Charge 91

INTRODUCTION

I celebrated a very special birthday for the first time in a long time a few years ago, and I remember a very strong prophetic word by one of my pastor friends at that time dealing with financial turmoil that was coming to the world, and the preparation we all can make towards it, both spiritually and financially. That financial turmoil manifested in the form of a deep recession according to economists late 2007 into 2008. As at the time of writing, there are still fears of further world-wide economic slowdown or even another recession, a term called double-dip recession.

After that celebration, I went about doing my normal day to day stuff, until the Lord started impressing me strongly to make some changes in my professional work. Eventually, I started obeying the Lord and from that came some trips outside of my home in Toronto, Canada. During one of those trips, the Lord started dealing with me about finances and as God would have it, I had the opportunity to minister in a church in Calgary, Alberta, Canada, and revelation exploded from there.

The Lord started speaking to me about the Blessing of the Lord, and how that blessing gives us a full supply. I taught generally about this scripture (Prov. 10:22) in Western Canada on a weekend, and travelled back to Toronto in the summer, and I decided to teach on this scripture at my home church, Harvest Miracle Christian Centre. As I started teaching on this, more revelation burst open, and I started seeing results in my own life of the word that I was teaching in greater dimensions. The Blessing of the Lord gives us a full supply, spirit, soul and body.

During this period, I was doing some work on my home driveway, and I extended the work to my neighbour's lawn, and I started complaining to the Lord why I have to do this little work for my neighbour, and he never does that for me. I was saying that I give and keep giving, but the person I am giving to is not showing any appreciation or giving me back in return. That little complaint turned into a conversation with the Lord, in which He expounded to me why I had to give and keep on giving, no matter the results, and He also showed me that one of the main pillars that have enhanced and helped me in my christian journey to date is the Spirit of Giving, and over the coming months, that revelation of the SPIRIT OF GIVING kept exploding in my life, hence the title of this book.

In this book, you would come to understand the SPIRIT OF GIVING, not just as another cute phrase, but as a revelation that would impart your whole life, including your spirit, soul and body and of course your finances too. This book would show you that giving is not just about money, but that Giving can be a Spiritual Force, that can unlock the windows of heaven on your behalf, and pour you out a Blessing that there would not be enough room to receive.

I strongly believe that those who are prepared and armed with the word of the Lord in these times would make it, despite the tough economic times. Functioning in the understanding of the SPIRIT OF GIVING, would have a lot to do with how we come out of these times with great testimonies. I believe that every financial hardship and failure is a test that can lead to a great testimony. Whatever your church tradition and denominational beliefs are, I want you to read the few chapters of this book with an open mind to receive and hear from the Lord, and to move forward and obey Him, in every way possible, so that you can receive all of your Harvest.

IN TIMES LIKE THESE

"And because lawlessness will abound, the love of many would grow cold. But he who endures to the end shall be saved. And this gospel of the kingdom shall be preached in all the world as a witness to all nations, and then the end will come. Mt. 24:12-14"

"But know this, that in the last days perilous times will come. 2 Tim. 3:1"

The Word says that in the last days perilous, terrible or difficult times would come. In many ways and for so many people, even born-again spirit filled, word confessing, tongue talking believers; these are very difficult times as prophesied in the word of God. The Word says that because iniquity shall abound, the love of many would grow cold. The Word also says that judgment must begin in the house of Lord. Tough times are here, and unfortunately would not be going away anytime soon, because it is the spirit of the last days. That is why we need to pray, and know how to stand in the midst of fiery trials, tribulations and temptations. The gospel is about good news, good news that we can be and we will be victorious in every of life's combat as believers in Christ Jesus. You cannot allow tough times to steal your joy. I know that a lot of people, even believers are facing tough times at home, in their family, with their children, in their marriages, in their work, in their business, in their physical body and to top it off a majority of christians are struggling financially and can barely make ends meet at the end of the week or at the end of the month, and literally have spent everything they have before they receive their routine pay checks. Let me just say this from the outset, that it has never been God's desire from time, for his people to live from pay cheque to pay cheque. That is a manifestation of the spirit of the curse on the land, but thank God we can rise above the curse and function in the Blessing of the Lord.

One thing we do know is that despite these difficult and perilous times, God is greater than every tough time that you have or will ever face. He is the way-maker, and He is revealing to those that are waiting upon Him, how to become fruitful and prosperous even in a dry and down economy. God wants us to function by the economy of heaven, and not by the ups and downs of Wall Street.

In times like these, you need to secure for yourself a strong and solid foundation built upon hearing and doing the word of God (Lk. 6:46-49). It is therefore pertinent to ask at this point, where and what is your foundation. Do you have a foundation of sand or the foundation of the rock? It is about time to build up, rebuild and solidify your foundation of hearing and obeying the revelation of God's word on a day to day basis.

First things first, get back to your foundation of God's word, and start building your life upon it again. Dust up your bible and start reading, studying and obeying the word of God because the Spirit of Giving is not going to work in your life without the solid foundation of the word of God.

The Spirit of Giving starts with making Jesus Christ, the saviour of the world, your Lord and personal saviour (Romans 10:9-10). It is time to call upon Him and be saved from your sins (Rom. 10:13). It is now time to make Him your personal Lord and Saviour. Now is the accepted time, today is the day of salvation. You are hearing his voice to come to Him today, do not harden your hearts. It is time to lay a solid foundation for your eternal destination with the Lord. The time to do so is now by praying this Prayer (Appendix A).

The Harvest is Here

Arise; shine; for your light has come! And the glory of the Lord is risen upon you. For behold the darkness shall cover the earth, and deep darkness the people; but the Lord shall arise upon you, and His glory will be seen upon you. Isa. 60:1-2.

We are in the last days, and as darkness covers the land (Isa. 60.1); and gross darkness the people, the light and the glory of the Lord is been revealed in His Church. We are the church of God's glory. The light of God is bringing revelation of the Harvest of these last days. The Word says the harvest is truly plentiful ... Mt 9:37. I have always pondered on this and in worship in church one day, I sensed in my spirit, the words, the Next Level is here. What is that next level, for me then and now, the next level is the Harvest. The Next Level is whatever you are believing God for, and expecting to happen in your tomorrow. Well, that future expectation is here.

The Spirit of Giving

As we see in John 4:34-38 Jesus is saying that we should look on the fields for they are white already for harvest (you do not have to wait for another 4 months). I say Amen to that because your field and my field are ripe already for harvest. He said to us we can reap where we did not sow. Others would labour and toil, and then God would bring you into their Harvest. What an awesome God. The harvest is here. You would have to release your faith for a NOW Harvest. Stop waiting around for a tomorrow harvest, the harvest fields are ripe already for a great harvest. Go ahead and reap the harvest fields that the Lord has for you in this season.

The manifestation of the glory of God, would lead to a great harvest of souls, and the purpose of kingdom wealth is to finance the harvest of souls and to advance the gospel of the kingdom of God to the nations of the world before the end.

Let us pray and let us believe together as the body of Christ in the earth for a greater manifestation of the glory of God, a greater harvest of souls into the kingdom of God, and greater release of finances in the hands of God's people for financing the end-time massive harvest of souls.

THE SPIRIT OF GIVING

"Give and it will be given to you: good measure, pressed down, shaken together, and running over will be put into your bosom. For with the same measure that you use, it will be measured back to you. Luke 6:38"

A lot of people give, but not so many have come into the place of the SPIRIT OF GIVING.

The Word says, that God so loved the world, that He gave his only begotten son, that whoever believes would be saved. So God gave His son, and the key is the love that caused Him to give His son. This popular scripture connects God's gift to mankind, as the manifestation of the love of God in action.

The Spirit of Giving

You cannot truly give, until you truly love. The Word says that God commends His love towards us, in that while we were yet sinners, Christ died for us, the righteous for the unrighteous (Rom. 5:8). The gift of Christ, the anointed one in His death and resurrection is a product of the love of God. Until you truly love, you cannot truly give. We can safely say then that giving is a by-product, or an outward manifestation of the Love of God in Christ Jesus. Functioning in the God kind of giving must therefore entail us functioning in the God kind of love.

Most of what we call love in the world today is for the most part unbridled selfishness and lust. Agape (the God kind of love) is actually kind, hopeful, enduring, patient, forgiving and for sure the key word is unselfish. The true love of God focuses on the benefit it can bring to bear on others, and not on the rewards and accolades, that it gets from others. It is about being a blessing to others and not trying to gain from others by every way possible. The passionate display of God's love must be to help, assist, minister to and meet the needs of others, and not just our own needs. If we truly love, our own needs must be secondary; our primary goal being to do what the Lord says we should do where others are concerned.

The Love of God, by which all men ought to know us as believers, becomes the motive of our giving. The Love of God, shed abroad in our hearts by the Holy Spirit (Romans 5:5, I John 3:17-18) becomes the core motivation for our giving. The Word is the foundation; the love of God is at the core of our giving. The drive for giving should come from the Love of God, not just in order to do a charitable act. That becomes the difference between worldly giving and godly giving.

Giving is the releasing of what you have, from a heart of the agape (unconditional and sacrificial) love of God, for the benefit of others, who may or may not have asked you. A lot of people would give to those that ask of them, and we ought to (Mt 5:42), but giving involves identifying needs, and moving forward in the ministry of compassion, to meet those needs wherever possible. For God so loved, that He gave … We ought to so love that we give from the overflow of the love that is in our hearts for others, that is what it means to love our neighbour as ourselves (Mt. 22:37-40). The heart of God's love is the heart that gives. The Word says that "… that He who did not spare His own Son, but delivered Him for us all, how shall he not with Him, freely give us all things …Rom. 8:32"

The body of Christ and our world in general is full of basically two groups of people where giving is concerned. There is one who scatters, and yet increases more; and there is one who withholds more than is right, but it leads to poverty. There are givers and there are takers. There are those who have the spirit of giving as we have been describing, and there are those that operate as takers. Givers are selfless and sacrificial, while takers are selfish, greedy and covetous. Givers are concerned more about others than themselves, while takers are more concerned about themselves than others.

The Spirit of Giving

I have always said that <u>JOY</u> means, <u>Jesus</u> first, <u>Others</u> second and <u>Yourself</u> last. You should love your neighbour as you love yourself, after loving God with all your heart, might, strength and resources. The love of God that you display towards your neighbour flows out of the reservoir of the love of God poured out in your heart by the Holy Ghost. It is time to go beyond ourselves in reaching out to others in the Love of God, that God demonstrated towards us, when He gave us Christ while we were yet sinners ... Romans 5:8. Givers flow in the blessings of the abundant supply of God Almighty, while takers languish in the curse of poverty ... Prov. 11:25-26. The curse in the Bible, in the times of the law and the prophets, was always threefold in manifestation: death, sickness and poverty. Thank God, we have been redeemed from the curse and the blessing of Abraham's covenant is ours in the new testament (Gal. 3:13-14,29), which means that we have been delivered from the curse of eternal death, sickness and disease, poverty, lack and impoverishment that resulted from sin, as we saw in the Old Testament (Deut. 28:14-61).

We see that givers function in the blessing (Deut. 28:1-13), while takers function in the curse of the law. Givers are on the side of obedience, while takers are on the side of disobedience, because the Word says that "Give and it shall be given back to you, pressed down, shaken together and running over ..." As we obey the Lord in the spirit of giving the blessing of the Lord overflows in our lives. If we would serve and obey Him, we shall spend our days in prosperity and our years in pleasures, says the Word, Job 36:11.

God is a Giver:

These scriptures and many more clearly demonstrate that Giving is God's idea in the human race. Giving is God's plan for our lives. He started and initiated Giving in the Garden of Eden, by creating Man, and placing him in the Garden of no want, a garden of abundance, and a garden of blessings,

The Spirit of Giving

where every human need was supplied in great abundance. God has always been the ultimate giver in the Universe, He has given the biggest gift of all eternity. His Son, Jesus Christ, being a very clear demonstration of the Love of God towards the human race. For God so loved, that He gave ... He is the ultimate in giving, and flows to us His grace and mercy without charge. Every good gift and every perfect gift is from above, and comes down from the Father of lights, with whom there is no variation or shadow of turning (James 1:17). What an awesome God, and how we are so grateful to God, that He is a Giver of Life, and the Source and Provider, from whom all graciousness and glory flows. He is the Father of glory.

He gave in the garden of Eden, He gave in the time of the law, He gave in the times of the Kings, He gave at the time of the prophets, He gave in the manifestation of His one and only begotten Son, Jesus Christ, He gave in the Acts of the Apostles, when the Holy Spirit was manifested, He has always given throughout all the ages. The amazing thing is that He is still giving today. He is still giving righteousness, peace and joy in the Holy Spirit today. He is still giving salvation, deliverance, healing and soundness. He is still giving life and life in abundance today. The thief (the wicked one, the devil) comes in order to steal, kill and destroy, but Jesus Christ came that we might have life, and life until it overflows (John 10:10). He is still giving Life today, even the God kind of life (Zoë), and as many as to come to Him for the God kind of life, He will in no wise cast out (John 6:37).

He gave His Son, who gave himself for us, that He might redeem us from every lawless deed and purify for Himself His own special people, zealous for good works. When the fullness of time had come, God sent forth His Son, born of a woman, born under the Law, to redeem (to deliver by paying a price) who were under the law, that we might receive the promise of adoption as sons. In the light of the spiritual reality that we are sons, God has sent forth the Spirit of His Son into our hearts, crying out, "Abba,

The Spirit of Giving

Father!" Therefore we are no longer slaves, but sons, and if sons, then heirs of God through Christ.

God is a Giver because God is Love (John 3:16). Love ultimately seeks to do well for the benefit of others, and we are ever grateful to God for His sacrificial love for us, that is the core of His Spirit of Giving, which we are beneficiaries of us. The heart of God is Love, which then leads Him to being the greatest and most perfect giver for time and for eternity. For the Lord God is a sun and shield; He will give grace and glory; No good thing will He withhold from those who walk uprightly (Psalms 84:11).

We are to be imitators of God in the Spirit of Giving, which we have seen in God. Freely we have received, freely we give. We give from the heart, motivated by the love of God (II Corinthians 5:14). The love of God in our hearts is the motivation, foundation and core of our Giving spirit. The Spirit of Giving flowing in us from the love of God kills selfishness in us, as human beings, for the love of God is not selfish. We do not look on our own needs but

The Spirit of Giving

on the needs of others. We look to God to meet our needs, and not to others. Our focus is to be a blessing, to others. We are not looking to take from others; we are always looking for opportunities to give and to be a blessing to others. We look unto God to meet and supply our needs according to His riches in glory by Christ Jesus (Phil. 4:19).

Human Selfishness Vs the Spirit of Giving:

For the most part, most of us live for ourselves and spend most of our time and resources on ourselves and our families, and for our immediate concerns. The Spirit of Giving calls upon us to go beyond the normal and allow the Spirit of the Love of God and the Spirit of Giving to build in us the character of selflessness. Human selfishness can cause us to spend a 100% of our time and resources on just ourselves, but God is calling us in the Spirit of Giving to go beyond and above ourselves and reach out to others, thereby dealing with the core of human selfishness within us. The Spirit of Giving transforms us, albeit gradually from the general lifestyle of human selfishness to the godly lifestyle of selfless service to our generation. It is time to cast off the spirit of selfishness, and to take on the mission of giving back to our generation, and becoming a force for good in the earth for the glory of the Lord, in these last days.

The spirit of poverty and impoverishment cannot continue to operate in your house if you function in the Spirit of Giving. As you distribute to others, you would be a continuously watered garden of the Lord. You are not meant to be a container of the blessings of the Lord upon your life, but a distributor of those blessings. You are not a warehouse of God's blessings; you are to be a fully functional distribution centre for the Lord, in terms of resources and blessings. Poverty, lack and impoverishment are a curse, and it is time to give it a boot from our lives by fully functioning and operating in the Spirit of Giving. Poverty diminishes us to less than who God made us to be, poverty humiliates the man and woman of

God, in us. Poverty devastates us, when we are left without the basic necessities of life.

We need to come out from under that burden and that yoke of poverty in the name of the Lord Jesus Christ. It is about time to live free from that wicked spirit that seeks to destroy us. We are coming out of the spirit and yoke of poverty, and we are coming into the spirit of giving, which would unleash in full force the blessings of the Lord upon our lives like we have never seen it before. The curse of poverty is broken, the Blessing of the Lord is being released now in the name of the Lord Jesus Christ.

We have identified two keys so far that should be at the foundation and core of our Giving. The word of God is the foundation for anything we are to do. The word of God actually says that if the foundation be removed what shall the righteous do? And everything we do as believers is a spiritual thing, even if they do not look, sound or feel spiritual. If you are going to function in the spirit of Giving, then the word of God has to be your foundation. You need to make your mind up, that you are going to believe what the word of God says above your tradition, culture, doctrinal or some kind of religious persuasion. You need to be convinced that you would adjust your belief system to conform to the clear cut revealed interpretation of God's word. As we go along we would confront some of these major beliefs that has held a majority of people in the shackles of poverty, but thank God revelation is coming and it is time to go free in the name of the Lord Jesus name. Amen.

The second key is the love of God, that is core motivation and spirit behind our Giving. The Love of God is pure and has no ulterior motives. That is the reason why you cannot carry evil thoughts towards others and have an unforgiving spirit, and function properly in the SPIRIT of GIVING. We would soon get into the Spirit of Giving proper, but suffice me to say, that most believers fail at these core foundational levels, and they try to build a house on sand, little wonder that it does not work. There is no if or but about it, Giving is not going to work, and in fact there would be nothing spiritual about it if we do not lay these proper foundations of the word of God and the love of God. I am amazed at how many people want to prosper in God that are living in unforgiveness even in their own families.

I very much doubt if the full manifestation of the spirit of Giving would unfold in a house or family or business that is divided, full of strife and contentions, with all kinds of arguments, fighting, and rebellious attitudes, dispositions and ungodly behaviours. It is time to repent, forgive and flow in the love of God in order for the word of God to work in our lives. The Word says we should be tender-hearted and forgive one another as God for Christ sake forgave us (Eph. 4:32), and that we should walk in the Spirit and not fulfill the lust of the flesh (Gal. 5:16).

In answering a question about what is the greatest commandment in Mt. 22:37-40; Jesus speaks here in answering the question about the Love of God; that loving God and loving your neighbour is the foundation on which all the law and the prophets function,

The Spirit of Giving

including the spirit of giving. It is very clear from these scriptures in Matthew and Luke; that foundational matters would play a major effect in us functioning effectively in the SPIRIT of GIVING.

Giving Involves Everything:

One of the greatest misunderstandings in this area of giving is that it is all about money. Money is a part of what we give but until we understand the true spirit of giving, then we miss the very essence of what God is teaching us here. Giving is first of all a spirit, before material things get involved. Of course we can give of our money, our time, our talents, and our skills. We can be hospitable to people, be kind and courteous, be generous, be forgiving, be tolerant and be patient with other people. We can also voluntarily donate goods and services to people without asking for any thing in return. In a relationship for example, we can give of our time, sacrifice for the other person, be there for one another and at times feel like we are the only one pouring into the friendship or marriage, while the other person does not seem to be doing anything or responding in kind. When we truly give, our lives are involved not just our money.

When we truly give from the heart of God's love it is sacrificial and for the benefit and good of others. It is my prayer that you catch and begin to function in the true complete life essence of giving and not just limit it to money or material goods and services. Money, material goods and services are just a part of the outflow of what I am calling in this book the true heart essence and spirit of Giving. It involves our whole lives, because if giving is not from the heart, it never truly blesses the other the person receiving from our giving.

THE BLESSING OF THE LORD

"The Blessing of the Lord makes one rich, And He adds no sorrow with it. Prov. 10:22"

To make rich is to have a full supply, enough to meet your needs and donate into every charitable endeavour that you desire to give to. According to Psalms 133 the blessing of the Lord is been compared to the oil that flowed from Aaron's beard as he was been consecrated as high priest of Isreal during their wilderness journey in the Old Testament. We know that oil stands for the anointing of the Holy Spirit, which produces life forever. We also know that the anointing of the Holy Spirit destroys yokes and removes burdens (Isa. 10:27). The phrase, The Blessing of the Lord is therefore the empowerment of the Holy Spirit – the anointing of the Holy Spirit to function in the life of God in us. That anointing produces life, peace and joy in us forever. The blessing of the Lord is the anointing and life presence of the Holy Spirit within us. The blessing of the Lord is the unction of the Holy Spirit that enables us to function spiritually and otherwise from the inside-out.

We can then see that the Blessing of the Lord is not the money, the cars, the houses, the miracles, the breakthroughs, etc but it is the anointing of the Lord within us and through us to produce supernatural results. The Blessing of the Lord is the 'I can do' spirit within us that in turn produces the blessings (the material stuff that we can see and hold) of the Lord upon our lives.

The Blessing of the Lord produces the blessings of the Lord in our day to day life. Therefore our focus should be removed from the blessings, and returned to The Blessing, and as we seek the Blessing and

The Spirit of Giving

increase in the blessing of the Lord in our lives, that power releases the blessings to meet and supply our needs according to His riches in glory by Christ Jesus.

The Blessing of the Lord is the spiritual force of favour in our lives (Psalm 5:12). The Lord is releasing a great dimension of favour upon His people in this season (Psalms 102:13) so that we can function spiritually to produce and manifest results in the natural realm of men.

The Blessing of the Lord causes the impossible to become possible (Luke 1:37, Mk. 9:23). The blessing of the Lord breaks down human barriers, obstacles, mindsets, hindrances and demonic strongholds and removes the oppression of the enemy. The blessing of the Lord causes bondages to be broken and sets us free from the oppression of our adversaries. The blessing of the Lord breaks through the natural realm to release miraculous manifestations of the Holy Spirit in the earth for the blessing of the people of God, and the world at large.

This is the time and this is the season to begin to walk in the Elisha's double portion of the blessing of the Lord in our lives. This is the time to seek, pray and begin to function in the greater anointing of the Blessing of the Lord. I believe that God is arising and having mercy (divine favour) upon the Church, Zion and His people, for the time for Zion to be favored, yes the set time is NOW. God wants us to begin to operate in the NOW blessing of the Lord, the NOW favour of God, to produce supernatural results in the natural, physical and earthly realm.

The Blessing of the Lord is the supernatural ability upon us, to produce supernatural results. He gives us the ability to make wealth, so that His covenant can be established in the earth (Deut. 8:18). He gives us wisdom, knowledge, witty inventions, supernatural insights and God-ideas that produce wealth at the practical level. The wealth of the sinner is laid up for the just (Prov. 13:22), and He turns over the labours and wealth of the unrighteous to the man who is good in His sight (Eccl. 2:26). The abundance of the sea shall be turned to you and the wealth of the Gentiles shall come to you (Isa. 60:5). The blessing of the Lord is the anointing of the Spirit of wisdom and understanding, the Spirit of counsel and might, the Spirit of knowledge and of the fear of the LORD (Isa. 11:2) upon our lives for not just spiritual breakthroughs and speaking in tongues, but also for supernatural wealth creation ideas, concepts and inventions.

The blessing of the Lord is the anointing for wealth and riches in the house of the Lord and it is light in the midst of darkness (Ps. 112:3-4), the anointing for supernatural increase (Ps. 115:14) and the anointing for supernatural multiplication (Deut. 1:10-11). In all that we do in this season, we should earnestly seek to be clothed with the Blessing of the Lord, which is the anointing of the Lord, the burden removing and yoke destroying power of God to produce supernatural ability, wisdom, knowledge, counsel and might in us, which otherwise who would not be able to function in. This becomes the most essential commodity and spiritual endowment and empowerment needed to conquer every spirit of lack, shortage, debt, insufficiency and financial handicap we may be currently facing. Let us believe the word of God for supernatural breakthroughs and divine restoration of everything that the enemy has stolen from us in these times as we also walk in the spirit and the power of giving.

THE SPIRIT OF LIBERALITY

There is one who scatters, yet increases more; and there is one who withholds more than is right, but it leads to poverty. The generous soul would be made rich, and he who waters will also be watered himself (Prov. 11:24-25).

The Word says that the liberal soul would be made fat and he that waters shall be watered also himself. Water is an essential ingredient for life individually and for the planet earth as a whole. If we can begin to function in the spirit and anointing of giving then we can be assured of being refreshed with the water of the word of God and the presence of the Holy Spirit. When we give we function in the God-kind of love (agape). Natural human thinking is selfish in its very nature but we experience great joy, happiness and fulfillment whenever we go against the grain of natural human thinking to release things to others. How about experiencing that joyful feeling all the time? Well that is possible if we decide to continually and consistently function in the grace of giving.

This grace of giving upon an individual is what I would call the spirit of liberality. Liberality is a disposition and an attitude of releasing of that which we own or possess. The purpose of this book is to teach us to get into the habit and mindset of always releasing and this is going to take a major shift in our minds to do this (Romans 12:1-2). As a man thinks so he is, so as you begin to reprogram yourself to come unto the giving side of life, your happiness, your joy and your fulfillment would be released, and then you can become a greater blessing to not just yourself but to others too. Always remember that life is not just about making yourself happy, but it is about pleasing God and making a whole bunch of other people around you happy also.

Some of us were brought up with little or nothing from a materialistic point of view, and if we are not careful as we grow and begin to make something out of our lives and prosper in God, that mindset of not having anything while growing up can lead us to develop a mindset of stinginess and selfishness, leading us not to freely give the way God has intended, for freely you have received, and freely you give (Mt. 10:8). We need to renew our thinking to break off from any mindset of holding on to everything we have got, because that would create a current of impoverishment in our lives. The spirit of poverty is not necessarily a lack of money but a mindset of holding on to everything you have got, and a stubborn refusal to release anything that would be of benefit to others and society around you. That refusal to release and thereby not flow in the spirit and anointing of the giving lifestyle would then release a current of lack and insufficiency in our lives.

The Spirit of Giving

I am a firm believer, that in order to break out of a mindset of poverty, break out from a natural human selfish spirit and to begin to function in the spirit of giving, we need to start giving away the top 10% of everything we make as the Lord's tithe starting from today. The Bible teaches that we should put this into the storehouse, which simply means the place from which we receive spiritual nourishment, which is your local church in this day and age (Mal. 3:9-10, Luke 11:42, Heb. 7:5-9). Most believers and christians know this tithing principle but never really practice it with any form of consistency, and wonder why they cannot truly make ends meet from a financial standpoint.

The Word says that we have been brought out of the kingdom of darkness and brought into the kingdom of His marvellous light (Col. 1:12-14). We now need to seek first the kingdom of God and his way of doing and being right (his righteousness) and all these things (the things others seek – food, clothes, houses, etc) would be added to us. To 'seek first' means to make something to be first place and first priority in our lives. For us to truly function in the spirit of giving, then we need to make (put) first place this tithing principle in obedience to the Word. God truly wants to be first in our lives and this tithing principle is a way to demonstrate our commitment to God and His word, and our willingness to break off from the mindset and spirit of poverty, lack and inability in our lives. Let us start to honour the Lord with the first fruits of all our increase so that our barns would be filled with plenty and our presses would burst forth with new wine (Prov. 3:9-10).

One of the things that would happen when we start doing this is that the spirit of selfishness would be broken over our lives as the more we give away, the less of a hold it has over our lives. Another thing that would happen is that we get into the habit of it, so it becomes easier and easier for us to do.

Tithing the tithe means praying over the tithe in worship, prayer and thanksgiving and declaring the faithfulness of the Lord in our deliverance from sin

The Spirit of Giving

and the oppression of the devil (Deut. 26). It opens up the windows or floodgates of heaven for us. God says He will rebuke the devourer and cause the floodgates of Heaven to be poured out towards us. We do need to live our lives under an open heaven so that our lives would be a true reflection of our heavenly Father. We need be like Joseph was in the land of Egypt. Before he even became the second in command in the land of Egypt, God caused him to prosper in everything he did even in prison and in Potiphar's house. He had the favour of God operating on his life everywhere he was. We need God's favour in day to day living, and the tithe opens up the floodgates of Heaven for us to walk in divine favour (Psalms 5:12).

One of the major things that hinder God's favour upon us, even in the area of the spirit of giving, is allowing the spirit of offence and unforgiveness to be in our lives on a continuous basis. Despite the many injunctions of God's word for us to forgive those that have offended us (Mk. 11:25, Eph. 4:32), many of us still hold on to past hurts and offences for long periods of times, thereby hindering the free flow of God's favour upon our lives on a daily basis. Refusing to forgive someone else either in a relationship, family, church, business or whatever the setting may be is one of the greatest tools the enemy is using these days to destroy not just individuals, but godly relationships, families and even churches.

We need to practice releasing people and not hold anything against them even after they have hurt us and offended us (Romans 12:14-21). I know it is not the easiest thing to do when we have trusted them so much, and then they turn around and break our hearts, but we have to rise above our hurts and wounds. We need to allow God to heal us and then flow in the grace of forgiveness towards others, because we cannot afford to stay under the spirit of offence as that would hinder the very light of the world and salt of the earth that we ought to be. Now is the time to forgive, do not push forward any more with unforgiveness, release everyone in your life now that has offended you, and where you know you have offended someone go ahead and speak to that person for forgiveness, so that you can experience the freedom and liberty of walking in the love of God. As much as lies in your power, live peaceably with all men.

Giving with the Right Attitude

Our priority where giving to God and giving to people are concerned is first of all, to advance the kingdom of God (Mt. 6:33). God does not want any soul to perish, so in order for the gospel to reach the nations of the world and to have the gospel preached every week even in our local churches, we need to give from the heart of the love of God. However God is not just interested in our giving, He is even more interested in the attitude with which we do it. He does not just want us to flow in the obedience of giving (Luke 6:38), but He wants us to do it with a cheerful or merry heart.

The Spirit of Giving

A cheerful heart is good medicine, and joy is a fruit of the spirit (Gal. 5:22-23). No matter what we may be going through, we should count every opportunity to give of our time, talents, money or resources as a time of joy and great celebration. Our attitude of giving would determine the altitude of results that our giving would produce. God has given us the oil of joy for mourning by His Spirit (Isa. 61:3). We are to draw waters from the well of salvation with the joy of the Lord (Isa. 12:3) and the joy of the Lord is our strength (Neh. 8:10).

We are to give with joyful celebration because God loves a cheerful and a hilarious giver. We are to give with laughter and great celebration. We are to give with our spirits up and our heads held up high. We are to give with our hearts and with great expectation and God is able to make all grace abound towards you, that you, always having all sufficiency in all things, may have abundance for every good work (2 Cor. 9:8).

The Spirit of Giving

There is a spirit of giving and that spirit of giving is the spirit of the joy of the Lord. Many of us never see our harvest of giving because we are not giving with rejoicing and celebration. For the most part we are giving just out of obedience, but it does take willingness and obedience to eat the good of the land (Isa. 1:19). We are not just to obey, but we are to be willing while being obedient. I do understand that at times, giving can be a great sacrifice and may even involve tears at times (Ps. 126) but we should always remember that today's sacrifices and today's tears would ultimately become tomorrow's joy because it is more blessed to give than to receive (Acts 20:35).

We need to fully understand there is a blessing to others and to us as we function in the spirit of giving, and we would be much better off doing it with joyful celebration. It is time to begin to flow in the joyful spirit of giving every time we have an opportunity to give.

GIVING PRODUCES RESULTS

The Word says we should cast our bread upon the waters, and we would find it after many days and we should sow our seed in the morning and in the evening, for we do not know which one the Lord would prosper. Most believers do function in the spirit and attitude of giving every now and then, but the critical ingredient of consistency is needed. Without diligence and consistency, which we can sum up in one word, faithfulness, we are not going to see the great results of giving. A faithful man would abound in blessings (Prov. 26:20). We need to become habitual, consistent, diligent and faithful

The Spirit of Giving

givers which mean functioning in the spirit of giving not just once in a while but all the time.

Giving ministers to others and it is a tool by which God ministers seed to those who need to sow and bread to those who need to eat (2 Cor. 9:9). Giving extends the hand of God to the poor, the widows, the fatherless, and all those in need of the basics of life. If any man counts himself to be religious, he ought to be ministering to the needs of the people around him. Giving is a product of the love of God in us for others. I do not believe we can truly love and not give. For God so loved the world that He gave (John. 3:16). We bring blessings to the people around us: family, church, friends, community, school, workplaces and all those in need that we do not even know when we flow and function in the spirit of giving. Our giving enables others to be able to function and continue to live life with the basic necessities of life.

Giving also blesses us because we are happy and joyful of being used to bless others. We need to flow in the gift of liberality (Rom. 12:8) and become distribution centres for the kingdom of God. It is time to step out of our containment system and get into the distribution system of God because that is where we can truly see fulfillment in our destiny and purpose in life. Without giving, we truly would live miserable and incomplete lives lacking in fulfillment and true joy in this earth. We are blessed in giving, as the Word says that it is more blessed to give than to receive. It is about time we begin to function in that greater blessing of being givers and not just receivers.

As we give to others, then others would also give to us (Luke. 6:38). Our motivation for giving should always be the love of God. For God so loved, He gave and the love of God constrains us (2 Cor. 5:14). However as we function in the spirit of giving, motivated by the love of God, certain things accrue to us as a result of being willing to obey the commandment of giving.

There has been a lot of misunderstanding in this area in the body of Christ. Some people have claimed that when we give to God, we are to expect nothing back from God in an attempt to criticize the teaching of giving to get. In an attempt to correct the teaching that the purpose and reason for our giving is to get they have brought an unscriptural teaching, that when we give to God we should expect nothing back in return meaning we should just give and forget about it.

First of all, the teaching of giving to get is correct in principle, the key word being correct in principle. The Word teaches that seedtime and harvest would not cease as long as the earth remains (Gen. 8:22), give and it shall be given to you and that whatever a man sows that shall he also reap (Gal. 6:7). In the light of these scriptures it is correct in principle to say that when do give, we should get just like the farmer who plants crops and sows seed should expect a harvest in due season. That is part of the universal law of sowing and reaping. That is a law, an established principle, which always works. Even people that are not christians practice the act of giving to get or better put, sowing and reaping, all the time. However

The Spirit of Giving

when it comes to God, our motivation for giving is not just to get, but is the love of God. We are giving because we love God and we love people, but at the same we are also obeying the laws of sowing and reaping, and giving and receiving. I think it is not wise for us to not expect those laws to work for us. In fact it is better that those laws work for us, so that the next time there is an opportunity to give, we can do so.

Everything in the kingdom of God works by faith (believing and acting on the word of God). So if we have no faith that the laws of sowing and reaping, giving and receiving would work for us, then we negate, limit and reduce the results that we are supposed to experience from obeying the giving and sowing part of the laws. Faith says that we receive what we confess according to the word of God (Mk. 11:22-24) which means if we do not believe and confess that the laws of sowing and reaping, giving and receiving are working for us, then we do not receive the results of our giving as we should.

The Spirit of Giving

Despite the fact that we love God, live holy lives, go to church regularly and give consistently we have to believe and confess the word of God concerning the laws of giving and receiving, sowing and reaping, seedtime and harvest, in order for those laws to work for us to the maximum. To continue to argue that we should expect nothing from God when we give is unscriptural and actually unwise, because eventually we would run out and not be able to give, and we also give the opportunity to the adversary to steal our harvest. Once again we are motivated by love in giving but by faith we should expect the results of giving to God to accrue to us according to the laws and established principles of giving that God has already set forth.

Another related area here is the giving of money, which is not the only thing that we can give. We can give time, our talents, prayers, words of encouragement, our love, our care, our resources, etc. Just giving someone a ride to and from church, and doing that joyfully, is to function in the spirit of giving. So giving is not restricted to money, though the giving of money is also an important part of giving to God and to others. We need to understand that the laws of giving and receiving apply to every area of giving, not just in the giving of money. If we give love, we would receive love, if we give friendship, we would receive friendship. Instead of complaining about what we do not have, the way to receive that is to actually give and sow in that area, so we then can receive a harvest in that area.

The important thing to realize here is get our motives right, and if our motives for giving or doing something is not the unconditional love of God, then we ought to check ourselves and bring ourselves into the love of God in that area.. One way to check that we are in the love of God is that when we do things for others, is it our expectation that the same people that we did the things for, would reciprocate us. Are we upset or angry that when we do something for others, and we get nothing back in return from the same people? You see, the love of God does not expect the results of giving back from the same people. Our expectation should be from the word of God and God who would raise men to reward us and give back to us, our expectation should not be from the recipients of our gifts, as for the most part they are not in position to give back to us.

The law of genesis says that every seed produces after its kind; just like in farming different crop seeds produce after their kind. Melon seed would produce a melon harvest, grape seed would produce a grape harvest, and collard green seed would also produce a collard green harvest. We do not expect a melon seed to produce an orange fruit, so it is universally accepted and according to the law of the first book of the Bible, Genesis, every seed produces after its kind (Gen. 1:12). It is amazing to me the many people who expect to receive different kinds of harvest, when they have not sown that kind of seed. The Word says God is not mocked, what you sow is what you reap. You cannot reap a financial harvest if you have not sown a financial seed. You cannot reap a harvest of a good marriage, if you have not sown the seed of being a good husband or wife, by not just words but actions of love, friendship, care and faithfulness. You cannot just expect to have great and faithful friends, who would be there for you in times of need, when you have not been a great and faithful friend, and been there for others at their times of need. You cannot expect to have a very good paying job if you have not applied yourself to educating yourself and improving your skills for the work place, so that you are able to actually do the job when God opens the door for you to have that job. If you are running a business, you should know as much as possible about that business, so that when God opens great business doors, we can actually walk into it and deliver on our client needs and customer expectations.

Most people in the churches today and in the body of Christ in general expect to just have things because they have prayed for it, but they forget that the laws of sowing and reaping also works for believers, and it is foolhardy to go and be asking God for financial breakthroughs, when you are not someone who gives your 10% tithe regularly and consistently, and in addition a giver of financial seed.

Now remember that every seed produces after its own kind, and financial seeds produce financial harvest. The whole idea that we can prosper in God without doing anything is leading to a lot of financial frustration in the body of Christ. The truth is that most regular church attendees are not doing well financially and the majority of prayer requests in church are for financial breakthroughs in addition to relationship issues. By the grace of God, I want to bring clarity and simplicity in this area of giving, so that the body of Christ and individual believers can have confidence in God's system, and actually work God's system and practically receive the results and benefits of it in their day to day lives. I know that this is possible if we can apply ourselves to it individually – nobody else can do it for you.

In addition, and very important, the quantity and size of our harvest depends on the quantity and size

The Spirit of Giving

of the seeds we sow and give. The harvest in God's kingdom does not work like the lottery where from the $5 dollar lottery ticket one person can win millions of dollars. The probability of you winning the lottery is so slim, that you may just want to cancel out of your plans and dreams for a jackpot and focus more on developing yourself in the spirit of giving. If we function in the spirit of giving, then it is in order and appropriate for us also to function in the spirit of and grace of receiving. It is quite alright to be blessed so much on our giving and receive the thirty-fold, sixty-fold and hundred-fold return according to our faith (Mt. 9:29). He that sows sparingly would reap sparingly, and those who sow bountifully would receive a bountiful harvest. We cannot receive a bountiful harvest from sowing sparingly. Once again, like a farmer, the size of the harvest depends on the size of the seed. That is the law and established principle (2 Cor. 9:6-10). If you are expecting the millionaire status then your giving should be in thousands. In other words base your expectations of your harvest on your seed. The role of prayer and faith is for you to receive the maximum harvest of the seeds that you have sown. This is how the law is set to work. It does not mean that God cannot supernaturally bless you without any seed, but that is left to God. In most cases, you have to function by His laws to get the right results. Do not just depend on a special move of God for you to receive the results of your giving, make up your mind to function in the laws of God, so that you can live in the results of willing obedience to the word of God on a day to day basis.

HEARING AND OBEYING HIS VOICE

As many as are led by the Spirit of God, they are the sons of God ... Rom. 8:14

My sheep hear my voice ... John 10:27

As we begin to function and flow in the spirit of giving according to the word of God, as we have been outlining in this book so far, we come to the place where we have become proficient and established in flowing in this area. Whether we feel like it or not and even when the conditions are not conducive, we have become habitual in our exercise of the Spirit of Giving. The creatures of habit that we are, we have now come to the place where the spirit of giving has become a part of us, just like not giving was a part of us before now. For some people, this may come naturally based on our upbringing and past lifestyle, but for others, this may take some time to build and develop. Whatever the case, it would really be worth it to develop the spirit and lifestyle of giving so as to become obedient to the word of God, and not just obedient, but obeying the word of God willingly.

As God would have it, we are now beginning to see the results of giving in our lives and the impact it is making in the lives of others, and also the impact of giving in the kingdom of God of which we are part of. So we are encouraged, we want to continue to do what we have mastered to do and to do it faithfully and consistently. We now begin to settle into the status quo of giving: we tithe, we give a certain amount of offerings, we are generous and we help others and donate charitably whenever we can, but that is just the foundation of the spirit of giving.

The Spirit of Giving

Having laid and started functioning in this dimension and level of the Word, God would now call us to a higher place and higher level of the Spirit of Giving. The Word says that those that have would have more given to them, and those that do not have, even the little they have would be taken away from them.

God is now challenging you to go to the next dimension of giving and to come to a place where you can be led by the Spirit of the living God in the area of the spirit of giving, as God begins to speak to you about how to give, when to give, who to give to and where to give. Those that would yield themselves to be used of God in this area of giving would now begin to hear and know the direction of the Lord not just in this area of giving but in every other area of their lives. The same Spirit of the living God speaking to you in this area would also open you up in every other area of your life thereby causing a revival of the word of the Lord in your life. The spirit of giving can cause you to hear and know the voice and leading of God in your life journey as you

The Spirit of Giving

learn to flow with the intuition and witness of the Holy Spirit in your inner man (Prov. 20:27). The Lord can then begin to teach you to profit according to the word of God and by the Spirit of the Lord (Isa. 48:17).

And as you obey the leading of the Word and the Holy Spirit (Deut. 28:1-2), then you begin to graduate and go to higher dimensions of it, that would in turn yield greater and mightier results until you practically begin to experience the exceedingly, above and beyond all you can ask or think according to the power of the Holy Spirit working on the inside of you (Eph. 3:20). Like the earthly mother of Jesus advised them at the wedding feast in Cana of Galilee (John 2:1-11), you are now being called upon to do whatever He says to you, especially in this area of giving as you have now become a willing and obedient distribution centre for the kingdom of God. The Lord can now faithfully rely and trust in you to carry out his giving wishes on the earth. That is indeed great company to be in, and it is literally available

The Spirit of Giving

to any one of us, that is willing to pay the prize and develop ourselves in this area. We have learned to trust the Lord and seek the face of the Lord and wait on Him and His leading in this and other areas of our lives (Isa. 40:31).

We should always remember that we are just stewards of God's resources, and the purpose of kingdom wealth is for the establishment of God's covenant and the advancing of the kingdom of God on the earth. As God begins to increase you beyond your wildest dreams even from a financial standpoint and as we begin to walk in and live out our dreams, we should remember to return all the glory to God, and not allow money, goods, things and material possessions to become idols and gods to us. We cannot serve and trust God and the spirit of mammon (the man-made world system of financial greed, selfishness and covetousness) at the same time. Money is just a tool for fulfilling God's mandate upon our lives and we should never allow it to change the people of God that we are. We should not become high-minded,

The Spirit of Giving

proud and arrogant because of material possessions (I Tim. 6:17). The Word clearly tells us it is hard for those who trust in riches to enter the kingdom of God and that the love of money (the wrong relationship with money) is the root of all evil.

God has called us to be His true worshippers in spirit and in truth (John 4:22-24) which means worshipping, serving and honouring him in every area of our lives. We should honour the Lord first with our lives, our conversation and our conduct as we seek to be examples of believers (I Tim. 4:12) in word, doctrine and purity. Our desire should be to please the Lord in every way we can, and not become a disgrace and shame to the name of the Lord. Without holiness no man shall see the Lord and be ye holy even as I the Lord I am holy (Heb. 12:13, I Pet. 1:16). We have been called to not only serve God in our giving, but also to be the light of the world and the salt of the earth, so that we can bring many with us into eternity with God through our Lord Jesus Christ.

The tendency is there as human beings, that as things begin to go well with us in every area, especially the financial area, we begin to do our own thing, start skipping church and all spiritual activities, stop tithing and giving generously, and then start living like lustful unbelievers, who acquire everything their eyes can see even when it is absolutely not necessary. God is not against us having the big cars and the big houses as we begin to prosper, but that is not what kingdom wealth is all about; it is about reaching people and changing lives and spreading the gospel to the nations of the earth. We definitely need the right balance and the right kingdom priorities, as God increases us more and more (Mt. 6:33). The kingdom of God must be the driving force of our lives, and not things and material possessions.

At the end of the day, the most important thing is that we make heaven and be with God for eternity. The fear of the Lord is the beginning of wisdom (Prov. 9:10). We must never allow any thing else (including material possessions and money) to take the place of God in our lives. We should not allow money and material possessions to jeopardize our relationship with God and God's people, compromise our faith and bring shame to the name of the Lord in the land. We must ensure that the money that was sent to be a blessing to us does not now become a curse to us, because of our misuse and abuse of it. We must have the right balance and the right place for money in our lives so that we do not make money the goal, driving force and passion of our lives. Money is just a tool for the establishment of God's covenant in the earth. We should not place our trust in uncertain riches but the only one true living God, the creator of the ends of the earth. Always remember that without holiness (right living and right conduct in accordance with the word of God), no man shall see the Lord.

RECEIVING BY GRACE

~

"Whatever you desire, when you pray, believe that you receive them, and you shall have them" Mk. 11:24

Everything we receive from God, we are going to receive it by grace through faith ... Eph. 2:9

At this point in this concluding chapter of this book I believe you have now come to a place of understanding the purpose and plan of God for your life, where Giving is concerned. It is also my desire that you have now made the decision or recommitted yourself to functioning in the Spirit of

Giving, according to the plans and purposes of God as set out in His Word.

The final frontier on the Spirit of Giving that we do not focus on a lot and is often neglected is the grace of receiving or in other words the Spirit of Receiving. One of the hardest things for believers to do is to receive from the Lord freely. We tend to feel that we have to pay something for it, as we say, 'if it is free, what is the catch?' The truth is that it is not free, it cost something, but thank God, Jesus in His death has paid the full price for it and God has accepted His death as full and complete payment. In addition, we at times feel that we should only give to God, and be sacrificial at giving, but as far as receiving is concerned we conclude that it depends on God, and that we play no active part in it. We often say that if God wants me to have it, He will work it out. Though it sounds very religious it is very unscriptural, as we do have a part to play it. There is a God-ward part to our receiving, which His grace has already provided, and there is a man-ward part, which has to come from us. Your financial destiny is not just up to God, it is also up to you, and you need to do your part because nobody else will if you do not.

Just like the farmer, who takes action and responsibility for sowing and planting; and also takes responsibility for reaping the crops when the harvest has come, we should also take responsibility for receiving the harvest from the seeds of giving that we plant. Once again, we need to take responsibility for putting in the sickle when the harvest is come (Mk 4:26). For example if a sinner does not take the action to accept Jesus as Lord and personal Saviour and believe that God has raised Him from the death for his justification, then he remains a sinner, bound for Hell unfortunately, despite the truth that the grace of God through the death of our Lord Jesus Christ has provided a means by which the sinner can become a born again believer, bound for a place called Heaven.

We do this by confessing (coming into agreement by saying the same thing as the Word). A word is

The Spirit of Giving

---

a thought expressed. To confess the word of God is therefore to speak the same words as what has been written in the Word. The Bible contains the expression of God's thoughts throughout the ages, and we come into agreement with God's word by confessing it with our mouth. Because faith comes by hearing and hearing by the word of God, we release faith each time we confess the word of God.

The grace of God (God's unmerited favour) provides salvation for us. Salvation means deliverance from sin, healing, soundness, preservation and wholeness according to the New Testament Bible concordance. Salvation provides for us in the covenant death, burial and resurrection of our Lord Jesus Christ, everything needed for eternal life and abundant life, to the full until it overflows. The grace of God brings salvation. We would not have salvation without the grace of God.

Everything we would ever desire according to the word of God is already provided for by grace, but we still have to receive it through faith. Faith is to believe in and act upon the word of God. It is also a practical expression of my confidence in God and in His word or my confidence in the love of God for me. We receive from God by grace through faith. Without the grace of God, all things needed for life and godliness would not be available to us. Thank God for the grace of God that spared not His only begotten Son, so that we can by Him receive all things. Grace provides it, but faith receives. Another great word for receiving is to take it. So we can say that grace makes it available, and faith takes it. For us to take the salvation, forgiveness, healing, deliverance and soundness that God has provided in His amazing grace, we need to walk by faith (an unseen spiritual force) and not by sight (the things which appear) for the things which we see are temporal or subject to change, but the things which we do not see are life eternal.

For us to develop our faith to receive from the Lord, we need to become proficient and habitual in our confession of the word of God over our lives.

The Spirit of Giving

That is how we take the things of God, even in this area of giving and receiving. The spirit of receiving is activated when we speak the Word consistently over our giving. Our giving is an act of worship to the Lord in spirit and truth (John 4:22-24). We need to also now begin to speak over our giving the word of God concerning giving and receiving so that our seed comes back to us as a mighty harvest as God has intended.

We need to be constant, consistent and diligent in this, because a lot of failures happen right in this area. We tithe, we give and we sow, and just expect that miracles would happen. Our harvest is out there because we have acted on the word of God and given; but we still have to call in that harvest into our bosom. If we do not call it in, it stays out there in the field wasting away and eventually destroyed. We need to take responsibility in this area and start activating the spirit of receiving and calling in our Harvest which is already ripe. This is your due season for your harvest. This is the time for you to reap of the seeds that you have planted all these many years. There is a lot of harvest out there for you, and the Lord is calling on you today to put in the sickle and reap this harvest.

Instead of complaining and grumbling about your shortage, lack and insufficiency, why not arise, and begin to flow in the spirit of giving, and in addition start confessing the word of God over your life and giving, so that results of giving flows to you rapidly according to the word of God. Do note that in most places where giving, seedtime, sowing are mentioned in the Bible, there is also a corresponding mention of reaping, harvest and receiving. God is our source and He is our supply for every need (Phil. 4:19), not the economy and any human being or human institution. The word of the Lord came to me many years ago that God has a divine supply for every human need. We just have to release our faith for it, and it is time to start doing so right now by speaking over our seed and calling into our lives the harvest of the seeds that we have sown.

Faith calls those things that are not as though they were (Rom. 4:17). God called Abraham the Father of many nations, before he even had an offspring. Faith calls into physical materiality the things that grace has provided in the realms of the spirit. We are already blessed with all spiritual blessings in heavenly places in Christ Jesus (Eph. 1:3). We need to start calling in those blessings into our lives in the right here and now.

There are different kinds of prayer (Eph. 6:18) and the Word says that we are to pray always with all manner of prayer or with different kinds of prayer based on the demand or the need, and there are different governing scriptures and principles on the different kinds of prayer. For example in the prayer of intercession, where we stand in the gap for others, we do persist in prayer and stand in the place of intercession, until we receive the breakthrough or until there is a release or the burden of prayer is lifted concerning that specific issue. However in the prayer of faith or the prayer of petition, when we ask and

The Spirit of Giving

receive from the Lord (Mt. 7:7-11) we believe that we receive the things we have asked the Lord for, at the same time that we asked him (Mk. 11:23-24). We cannot apply the rules of the prayer of intercession to the prayer of asking and receiving and vice-versa. We need to fully understand how all these different kinds of prayer work and function so that we get the desired results according to the word of God.

The spirit of giving and receiving is in the arena of the prayer of asking and receiving, where we need to apply our faith, at the point of giving and believe that we receive our harvest when we give. We continue to water our seed by the confession of the word of God consistently and continually over our giving. It is important we also operate in the fruit of patience (Heb. 6:12) so that we do not give up, quit or grow weary in the time and season of waiting for physical manifestations; that at times, could delay; and one of the things that contribute a lot to delays is our up and down confession while we wait for the manifestation of the promises of God in our lives. We have to maintain a consistent confession of faith through this perhaps most difficult season between giving and receiving, sowing and reaping, seedtime and harvest. We cannot afford to grow weary in well-doing for in due season we shall reap if we do not faint (grow weary, quit and give up). The harvest truly is plentiful and due season always comes.

I believe that in this season, we would see the harvest come more quickly as we stand to faithfully, conscientiously and diligently declare the Word over our lives and our every seed (which also represents our lives, our time, our investments and the labour of our hands) to come forth in manifold, multiplied and increased harvest so that we truly come to a place of being able to support and advance the kingdom on so many needed fronts. This is the time, this is the place, and this is our due season. Let us get it done church. It would be by grace, not by our own righteousness, and it will be through faith in the name of the Lord Jesus Christ. Amen.

CONCLUSION

Having read this book on the spirit of giving, I believe that you have come to know and understand that God is a giver, and have placed in each one of us the desire to flow, function and operate consistently and faithfully in the spirit of giving.

It should be established by now that God not only wants us to give, but to give with an attitude of joy and hilarious celebration, in a way that pleases God, from our heart of love for Him and His kingdom, and to others also in order to be a blessing to those in need all over world, starting from our immediate communities. God promises to repay anyone that lends to the poor. Bear in mind that God is the One that repays us, as the poor do not have the ability to repay us.

It is very scriptural to expect by faith the maximum results that God has promised us as we obey His word and the laws that he has set concerning the spirit of giving. We cannot develop and master the spirit of giving until we set out to be givers in our day to day lives in every area possible as God enables us with great grace. It has been the purpose of this book to not just teach us to be givers in every area of our lives, but to impart to us the spirit of giving, as it is my firm belief that giving is a spirit, flowing from God, that has the power if applied according to the word and laws of God, to completely eradicate every spirit of poverty, lack, insufficiency, shortage in our present lives and experience.

While giving is not restricted to money, the laws of giving also apply to money and there is no other short-cut to financial prosperity in the kingdom of God but through the principles of seedtime and harvest, giving and receiving, sowing and reaping. The diligence, faithfulness and consistency with which we apply these laws in the financial area would determine our financial destiny even in the midst of an uncertain economy.

You need to change your thinking from a mindset of lack and insufficiency to a mindset of abundance and prosperity because God wishes that we prosper and be in good health according to the prosperity of our souls, which includes our will, mind and emotions (3 John 2). We have to be transformed by the changing of our minds as a butterfly metamorphoses, because as a man thinks in his heart so is he (Prov. 23:7). As we give to God, motivated by His love, as individuals and as the body of Christ in this season, we must now begin to fully embrace and believe for the results of our giving, as the farmer fully takes ownership of reaping his crops after a season of planting and sowing. We need to change our minds to agree with becoming prosperous and wealthy in God, for the advancement of the kingdom of God and for the blessing of the nations.

The Spirit of Giving

The preaching of the gospel in our generation according to the Great Commission (Mt. 28:18-20, Mt 24:14) and through every available media voice and outlet cost a lots of money in this generation, and believers have to prosper enough to be able to take care of themselves and their families, and cater to the greater and larger vision of supporting and advancing the preaching of the gospel to the nations. Kingdom prosperity according to God's system should not just be a lingo that we are upset at and angry at because we are afraid people would become money-minded and covetous, but should become a rallying cry for us to take our place in God and become everything God has called us to.

An action plan for believers to start with includes repentance and a firm and quality decision to now become givers. We need to accept the message of giving with the results that follow, and not be afraid of covetousness and greed, as we obey the word of God and function in the laws and principles of giving that God has set.

The next step in this action plan is to start with the tithe (Prov. 3:9-10). We need to honour the Lord with our first fruits. If we keep saying we cannot afford to tithe because we are coming short every month, then we would keep coming short every month and never come out of shortage and lack. There is no point tithing with the wrong attitude. The tithe enables us to have the devourer rebuked and the windows of heaven open for us (Mal. 3:9-10).

We need to live and operate under God's open heavens. Another translation says the floodgates would be open unto us, as we bring the tithes and offerings into God's house. It is not just the tithe, but the tithe and in addition to the tithe, the offering. The tithe is our defensive seed for protection from the devourer, and the offering is our offensive seed for the floodgates of heaven to be open to us for us to increase and prosper supernaturally. As we tithe the tithe and give our offerings, God has promised to so open the windows and floodgates of heaven, such that there will not be enough room to receive the

The Spirit of Giving

outpouring of the harvest. Until you become a consistent and faithful giver in the area of the offering in addition to the tithe, it is my firm belief that you cannot truly prosper in God according to the word and principles enunciated in this book from the word of God.

If we are faithful, diligent and consistent in the tithe, and in addition the offerings, as we are directed by the Lord, with the clear understanding of the word of God and function in the spirit of giving as outlined in this book, I believe that in a period of one full year, which is the time of the natural season of sowing and reaping in the natural, we can experience a complete turnaround for the better where our lives in general and our financial lives are concerned.

I prophesy unto you that it is time for you to move from the low place of lack, insufficiency, shortage and impoverishment and move up to the higher place of prospering in the kingdom in God in every area of your life, including finances. I truly believe that is the will of God for your life and destiny in this season. Indeed the curse is broken and destroyed; the Blessing of the Lord is released in your life. That Blessing of the Lord that is being released in your life now makes you rich (have a full supply) and adds no sorrow to it in the name of the Lord Jesus Christ. The name of the Lord is been glorified in your life. Amen and Amen.

THE CHARGE

As you begin to prosper in God, which you will, as you follow these godly principles, I want to leave you with a charge to go make the world a much better place. If you follow the news at any level, you will see that people and communities around you and abroad are in great need. With the recent economic recession, a lot of needy people are without any means of livelihood and the generosity of a lot of people that have been giving previously has been impacted. There is just so much suffering around you, and you should not just take notice but need to do something about it. If it is touching your heart, then you are been called upon to take action.

The Spirit of Giving

One of the primary reasons that God has brought this timely word for you is to prosper you, and as you do prosper, please join me to extend a helping hand to the needy, dying and suffering masses around the world, especially in needy continents like Africa, Asia, Central America, South America and even in some parts of Europe, Australasia and North America. We all need to join and give to and invest in reaching the homeless, hungry, destitute and orphans around the world. God is calling us all to give to those in need around the world as a mark of true religion (Eph. 4:28, James 1:27) and to help us to take the gospel around the world from a heart of love and compassion (Mt. 9:38-40).

It is my prayer that you would heed this call as you partner with us and with godly agencies around the world to touch a dying world with the gospel and by ministering to their spiritual, physical, and emotional and financial needs also. Remain Blessed in the Lord and remember that it is God's will for to prosper and be in health, even as your soul (mind, will and emotions) prospers in the name of the Lord Jesus Christ. Amen.

APPENDIX A

PERSONAL PRAYER TO BECOME A BORN AGAIN BELIEVER

My Heavenly Father, I thank you for sending Jesus Christ, to die for my sins on the cross of Calvary. I accept His sacrificial death as the full payment for my sins and the penalty of death for me. Amen.

I repent of all my sins. I confess with my mouth that Jesus Christ is Lord, and I believe in my heart that God has raised Him up from the death for my justification. I make Jesus Christ my Lord and my personal saviour from this day forward. Amen.

The Spirit of Giving

I accept his forgiveness and receive His Holy Spirit to be my teacher and guide. I am now born again and I have passed from death to life and according to the Word, my name resides now in the book of life. Lord teach me to pray, to live each day for you by reading your Word, and to find a good Bible believing church that preaches and teaches your Word in the name of the Lord Jesus Christ. Satan, the devil is no longer the Lord of my life, and Jesus has now become my Lord and personal saviour. Amen.

I congratulate you today on making the commitment to follow the Lord Jesus Christ as His disciple. I believe that this is the beginning of greater things in your life, as you lay a solid foundation for yourself in these times. The word of God and prayer would be great assets to you or as you begin or re-launch your christian journey at this time. The word of God would give you a solid foundation on what God is saying, and prayer would be a medium for you to communicate back to God what you are learning in the Word and fellowship with Him on a day to day basis. You also need to start attending a Bible-Believing (Word-based) church that would teach you to grow in the grace and knowledge of our Lord Jesus Christ.